THE STORY OF THE
CAROLINA PANTHERS

NFL TODAY

THE STORY OF THE CAROLINA PANTHERS

MICHAEL E. GOODMAN

CREATIVE EDUCATION

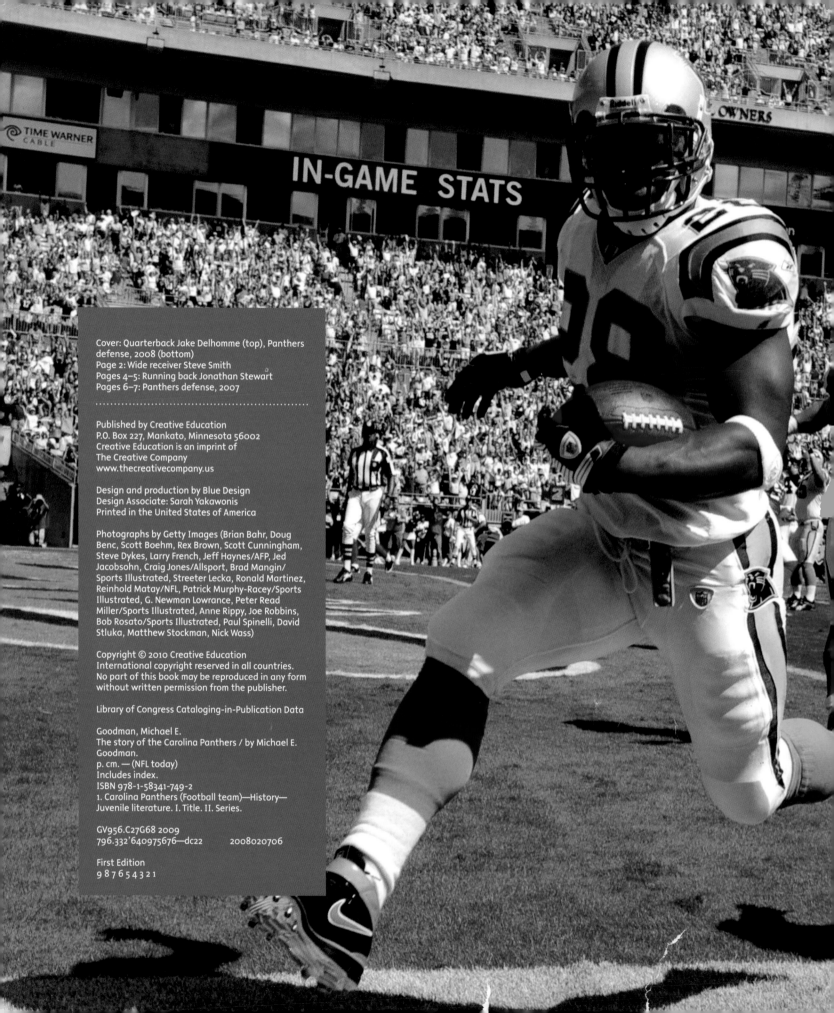

Cover: Quarterback Jake Delhomme (top), Panthers defense, 2008 (bottom)
Page 2: Wide receiver Steve Smith
Pages 4–5: Running back Jonathan Stewart
Pages 6–7: Panthers defense, 2007

....

Published by Creative Education
P.O. Box 227, Mankato, Minnesota 56002
Creative Education is an imprint of
The Creative Company
www.thecreativecompany.us

Design and production by Blue Design
Design Associate: Sarah Yakawonis
Printed in the United States of America

Photographs by Getty Images (Brian Bahr, Doug Benc, Scott Boehm, Rex Brown, Scott Cunningham, Steve Dykes, Larry French, Jeff Haynes/AFP, Jed Jacobsohn, Craig Jones/Allsport, Brad Mangin/Sports Illustrated, Streeter Lecka, Ronald Martinez, Reinhold Matay/NFL, Patrick Murphy-Racey/Sports Illustrated, G. Newman Lowrance, Peter Read Miller/Sports Illustrated, Anne Rippy, Joe Robbins, Bob Rosato/Sports Illustrated, Paul Spinelli, David Stluka, Matthew Stockman, Nick Wass)

Library of Congress Cataloging-in-Publication Data

Goodman, Michael E.
The story of the Carolina Panthers / by Michael E. Goodman.
p. cm. — (NFL today)
Includes index.
ISBN 978-1-58341-749-2
1. Carolina Panthers (Football team)—History—Juvenile literature. I. Title. II. Series.

GV956.C27G68 2009
796.332'640975676—dc22   2008020706

First Edition
9 8 7 6 5 4 3 2 1

IN-GAME STATS

TIME WARNER CABLE

OWNERS

CONTENTS

ON THE SIDELINES

MEET THE PANTHERS

EXPANSION
EXCITEMENT

X------------------------------

In 1663, King Charles II of England gave a large area of land that extended from southern Virginia to northern Florida to a group of eight wealthy plantation owners. The owners named the colony Carolina, a Latin version of the name Charles, to honor the king. In 1729, Carolina was divided into two sections that later became two states. While each state today has its own identity, the two have maintained close connections over the years.

A new connection was established in 1993, when the National Football League (NFL) awarded an expansion franchise to the region. Team owner Jerry Richardson, a former NFL player who was raised in North Carolina but attended college in South Carolina, wanted the team to represent both states. Hoping the club would demonstrate the speed and power of a big cat, Richardson named it the Carolina Panthers.

Richardson began making plans to bring a professional football team to the Carolinas in 1987. That was when NFL owners announced a competition to determine where to locate two new franchises. Richardson and his son Mark, a financial expert, approached several business executives in Charlotte, North Carolina, and convinced them to be part of a funding plan for a regional Carolina team.

Richardson was well known in the area as both an outstanding football player and a successful businessman. In the late 1950s, he was a star wide receiver at tiny Wofford College in Spartanburg, South Carolina. He then played for two years with the Baltimore Colts and caught a touchdown pass in Baltimore's 31–16 victory over the New York Giants in the 1959 NFL Championship Game.

Using the $4,744 he received as a winner's bonus from that game, Richardson bought one of the first Hardee's fast-food restaurant franchises, which he opened in Spartanburg in October 1961. He then retired from football to concentrate on what would become a very successful business career.

Over the next 25 years, Richardson often dreamed about becoming the owner of a professional football team. He saw his opportunity to make that dream come true when the NFL announced its intention to expand in 1987. Richardson worked for the next several years to develop a solid business plan that convinced the league to award a franchise to the

JERRY RICHARDSON

TEAM FOUNDER, OWNER
PANTHERS SEASONS: 1995-PRESENT

Jerry Richardson always set his goals high and worked hard to achieve them. Even competing far from the spotlight at Wofford College in Spartanburg, South Carolina, he believed he could play professional football, and he achieved that goal. Then, when the Baltimore Colts refused to give him the $250 raise he felt he deserved, Richardson left football to concentrate on his business career. Starting with one South Carolina-based restaurant in 1961, Richardson and his partners built an empire of more than 2,500 restaurants that employed 100,000 people. Then he turned his sights back on pro football in the 1980s, determined to bring an NFL franchise to the Carolinas. "This region and its people have been so good to me and my family that there was never any question of what I wanted to do. My dream was returning something to this special area," he said. Traditionally, the Carolinas have been better known for college basketball than pro football, but the Panthers quickly developed a strong fan base. Richardson's leadership and vision earned him a place in the South Carolina Business Hall of Fame in 2006.

ON THE SIDELINES

PLEASE TAKE A SEAT

Although Jerry Richardson may have been the guiding force in establishing the Carolina Panthers franchise, the people of North and South Carolina played a major role in convincing the NFL that the region really wanted this new club. Here's how: Richardson told local citizens that a proposed stadium in Charlotte would be financed without using any public tax dollars. Instead, personal seat licenses (PSLs) would be sold to raise most of the money. Purchasers had to agree to pay thousands of dollars for the right to buy season tickets in the new stadium in addition to buying the tickets themselves. Richardson and the league wondered if Carolina citizens would support the PSL concept. The answer came quickly. July 1, 1993, was set as the first day for accepting orders for PSLs. By the end of that day, an amazing 41,632 PSL orders had been received. By September 3, nearly 50,000 PSLs had been purchased, and a total of $112.7 million was pledged for the new stadium. Impressed by the public's level of commitment, the NFL awarded the franchise to the Carolinas two months later.

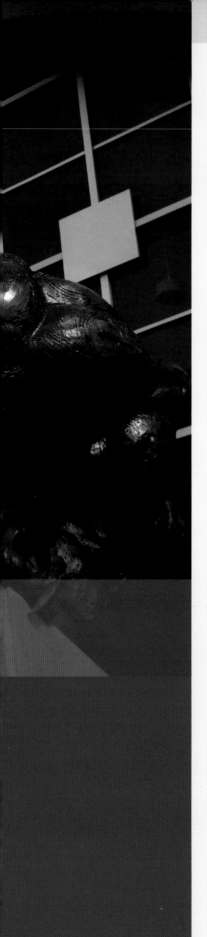

Carolina Panthers. The team was scheduled to begin league play in 1995.

The club now had a name, but it needed a stadium, a coach, and players. Under Richardson's direction, plans were drawn up for a state-of-the art stadium to be built in downtown Charlotte. The stadium wouldn't be ready until the 1996 season, so the Panthers would spend their first year playing home games at Clemson University in Clemson, South Carolina. Richardson then hired veteran football executive Bill Polian as general manager and put Polian in charge of selecting a head coach and players for the new club.

Polian interviewed several coaching candidates before making an offer to Pittsburgh Steelers defensive coordinator Dom Capers. What most impressed Polian about the 44-year-old Capers was his work ethic—no one put in more hours working on the field or studying game films than Capers. "Football is a way of life," Capers once said. "However long it takes to get the job done, we'll do it. The most important thing is for us to be as well-prepared on Sunday as we can be."

Working together, Polian and Capers assembled the first Panthers roster. Choosing from a list of players made available from the other NFL teams in an expansion draft, Carolina selected such proven talents as cornerbacks Rod

Smith and Tim McKyer, receiver Mark Carrier, and defensive tackle Greg Kragen.

The Panthers' front office next looked to the 1995 NFL Draft to find a young quarterback to lead the team's offense. Their choice was rocket-armed passer Kerry Collins, who had piloted Penn State University to an undefeated season in 1994. Collins had impressed many talent scouts with his size, arm strength, leadership skills, and poise.

The team still had many holes to fill, so Polian signed several veteran free agents, including linebackers Lamar Lathon and Sam Mills, safety Brett Maxie, and placekicker John Kasay. These players made up a solid veteran core for the new team, which played its first game on September 3, 1995, against the Atlanta Falcons.

The Panthers lost that first contest 23–20 in overtime and were defeated in their next four games as well. But then they began a remarkable turnaround. The Panthers pounced on 7 of their next 11 opponents, including the defending Super Bowl champion San Francisco 49ers. The club finished the season 7–9, which was the best record ever for a first-year NFL team. Excited Carolina fans wondered just how far this special new team could go. They would soon find out.

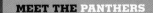

KEVIN GREENE

LINEBACKER
PANTHERS SEASONS: 1996, 1998-99
HEIGHT: 6-FOOT-3
WEIGHT: 247 POUNDS

When Dom Capers was defensive coordinator for the Pittsburgh Steelers, the one player he never had to push to be aggressive on the field was linebacker Kevin Greene. In his first 11 NFL seasons with the Los Angeles Rams and the Steelers, Greene established himself as one of the best in the league at sacking quarterbacks and at causing and recovering fumbles. That's why he was named to the NFL's All-Decade team for the 1990s. No one hit opponents harder than Greene, and no one was as adept at pouncing on loose balls. "It's the intensity of his play that puts him in position to make those fumble recoveries," said Capers. "Throughout his career, he's always been trying to get to the ball." That's why the Panthers' coach urged team management to sign Greene as a free agent prior to the 1996 season. Greene played two Pro Bowl seasons in Carolina and was named Linebacker of the Year by the NFL Alumni Association in both 1996 and 1998. Off the field, Greene had a second aggressive career—as a professional wrestler.

SOPHOMORE
SENSATIONS

X----------------------------------

If the Panthers' first-season results were surprising, their second-year performance was astounding. The club opened the 1996 season in the brand-new, 73,000-seat Ericsson Stadium in Charlotte (which was renamed Bank of America Stadium in 2004). The entrances to the new field were guarded by six massive bronze panthers whose fierce expressions let visiting teams know they were in for a fight. "I love the big cats," said Carolina offensive tackle Blake Brockermeyer. "They make the place look mean."

Opponents soon learned just how mean the Panthers could be in their new home. Carolina went undefeated in eight regular-season games at Ericsson Stadium on its way to a stunning 12–4 record. Playing in front of sold-out crowds, the Panthers usually blew out opponents by double-digit margins. "From the time you walk into this place, you feel invincible," said Panthers linebacker Kevin Greene. "The fans won't let us lose."

The Panthers finished the 1996 season with seven straight wins and roared into the playoffs. As the winner of the National Football Conference (NFC) West Division, Carolina earned a bye in the first round of the playoffs. Then, in the second round, the Panthers defeated the Dallas Cowboys 26–17 to earn a spot against the powerful Green Bay Packers in

the NFC Championship Game. "Here's a team that wasn't even
a team three years ago," said sportscaster John Madden,
"and now they are just one game away from the Super Bowl."

Playing in below-zero temperatures in Green Bay,
Wisconsin, the Panthers couldn't get their offense revved up,
and their Super Bowl dreams ended with a 30–13 defeat. "This
was one time when home-field advantage really counted,"
said Jerry Richardson.

After the Panthers' sensational sophomore campaign,
Carolina fans were hoping for even greater achievements
in Ericsson Stadium in the late 1990s. They were soon
disappointed, however. The Panthers' record slipped to 7–9
in 1997 and then to 4–12 in 1998 after injuries and player
disputes destroyed the team's winning chemistry.

Collins, who began to struggle with alcohol abuse
problems, was released midway through the 1998 season
and replaced by veteran Steve Beuerlein. Although Beuerlein
made a strong showing, the Carolina defense had a terrible
year. After the season, Capers was fired as head coach and
replaced by George Seifert, who had previously led the 49ers
to two Super Bowl wins.

Looking over his new team, Seifert was impressed with
some of the offensive talent already in place. This included

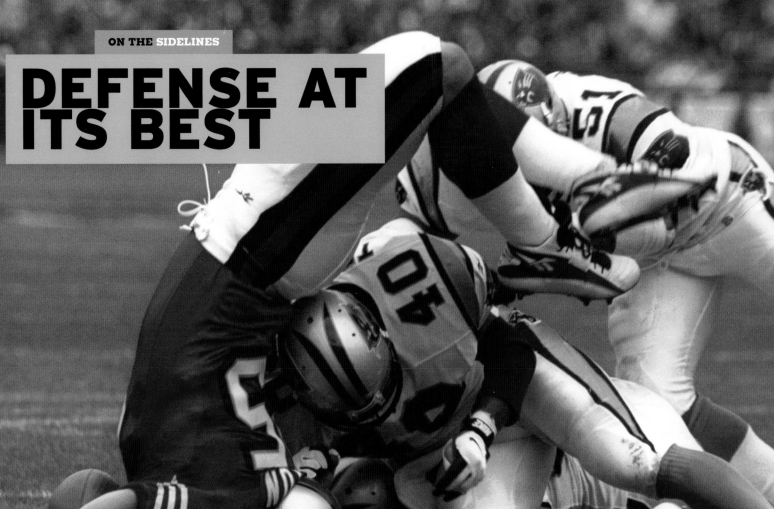

DEFENSE AT ITS BEST

The Panthers shocked most football experts by capturing the NFC West Division crown in 1996. Using a smothering defense designed by coach Dom Capers, the Panthers gave up more than 20 points only twice that year. So it is not surprising that the season's most important play occurred on defense. Carolina needed to defeat the powerful Pittsburgh Steelers in the final regular-season game to claim the division title and earn a first-round bye in the playoffs. Pittsburgh got off to a 14–9 first-half lead. Then Carolina bounced back in the second half with three John Kasay field goals to move ahead, 18–14. In the final minute, the Steelers drove inside the Panthers' 10-yard line. Carolina defenders stopped three straight Pittsburgh plays cold. With only 29 seconds left, Steelers quarterback Kordell Stewart spotted a receiver in the back of the end zone. His pass was on target, but Panthers safety Chad Cota jumped in front of the receiver to intercept the pass and seal the victory. "That play was a fitting ending," Capers told reporters. "It showed the strength of will of our guys."

Beuerlein, tight end Wesley Walls, and wide receiver Muhsin Muhammad. Coach Seifert also saw the makings of a strong defense in such players as linebacker Michael Barrow, safety Mike Minter, and tackle Sean Gilbert.

After the Panthers got off to a 2–5 start in 1999, Seifert decided to stir up the team's offense by employing the "West Coast Offense" attack his 49ers teams had used so successfully. Beuerlein began throwing short passes all around the field, completing 343 of 571 tosses for 4,436 yards and 36 touchdowns. The new offensive strategy turned the season around, and the Panthers won six of their last nine games, finishing with an 8–8 record and barely missing the playoffs. "It was a great run for us," said Beuerlein. "A lot of people wrote us off early in the year, but our guys kept scrapping."

FOLLOWING FOX
TO VICTORY

Unfortunately, Coach Seifert was unable to achieve the same success in Carolina as he had in San Francisco. His Panthers played inconsistently in 2000, finishing 7–9. Then, in 2001, everything fell apart. The team underwent a shakeup before the season when Beuerlein left town as a free agent. Rookie quarterback Chris Weinke led Carolina to an opening-week victory over the Minnesota Vikings, but that turned out to be the team's only win of the season. Over the next 15 weeks, the Panthers suffered late-game collapses, overtime losses, and occasional blowouts. At the end of the 1–15 season, Seifert resigned.

While the Panthers collapsed in 2001, the New York Giants were coming off a Super Bowl appearance, thanks in large part to the direction of their defensive coordinator, John Fox. Before the 2002 season, the Panthers hired Fox to replace Seifert as head coach. Coming into his first Carolina training camp, Fox told his players that he expected them to do two things—work hard and have fun. But then he

NFL TODAY: THE STORY OF THE CAROLINA PANTHERS

Stephen Davis was used mainly as a blocking fullback early in his NFL career with the Redskins, but he was recognized as an elite ballcarrier by the time he joined the Panthers in 2003. **X**

MEET THE **PANTHERS**

JOHN FOX

COACH
PANTHERS SEASONS: 2002-PRESENT

When John Fox took over the Panthers in 2002, the team was coming off a one-win season. Over the next five years, he guided the club to two playoff appearances, two NFC Championship Games, and a Super Bowl. Like their coach, Fox's Panthers squads became known for their hard work and confidence. They almost never lost a close game. The secrets to Fox's success lay in his ability to communicate with his players and to drive them to excel. "He criticizes in a way that's funny," said Giants cornerback Jason Sehorn. "He tells you what you're doing wrong and picks you up at the same time. Players like and respect that." A defensive genius, Fox quickly turned the club around. In 2002, the Panthers ranked 5th in the NFL in overall defense, improving from 28th the previous year. The following year, they completed their turnaround by making it all the way to the Super Bowl. "The best thing about John," said former NFL coach Jim Fassel, "is that he acts like he's having fun, and his energy transfers to the team."

repeated one of his favorite quotes: "This game is only fun when you win."

A masterful defensive tactician, Fox aimed to build a winner in Carolina by first focusing his attention on defense. The Panthers possessed the second overall pick in the 2002 NFL Draft, and they used it to acquire All-American defensive end Julius Peppers from the University of North Carolina. Peppers had great size (6-foot-6 and 283 pounds), and his intense style on the field reminded many fans of former NFL defensive great Lawrence Taylor, who had also starred at the University of North Carolina. "Peppers is probably the most athletic guy I've played with since I've been in the league," said veteran defensive tackle Brentson Buckner. "You have a guy in a defensive lineman's body who has feet like a defensive back and the speed of a safety."

Led by Peppers on defense and veteran quarterback Rodney Peete and receivers Muhsin Muhammad and Steve Smith on offense, the Panthers got off to a quick start under their new coach's leadership, winning their first three games. Then they suffered a series of devastating injuries and lost eight straight contests. Carolina fans feared that the 2002 season might turn out to be as depressing as 2001 had been. But the team staged a late-season rally to finish with a respectable 7–9 record.

With Peppers as the cornerstone, Coach Fox changed the Panthers' defense from one of the NFL's worst into one of its best. He also began focusing on ways to improve the offense, signing powerful running back Stephen Davis, sure-handed wide receiver Ricky Proehl, and talented but inexperienced quarterback Jake Delhomme before the 2003 season. Fox knew he would be taking a chance in handing the team's offensive reins over to Delhomme, who had seen little

RUN, STEVE, RUN!

During his pro career, quarterback Steve Beuerlein was noted for his throwing arm but not his running ability. Yet a Beuerlein run ranks as one of the most memorable plays in Panthers history. It occurred during a game against the Green Bay Packers in December 1999. With only five seconds to go, the Panthers, trailing 31–27, had the ball on the Green Bay five-yard line. There was time for only one more play. Coach George Seifert called Beuerlein to the sidelines and suggested a quarterback draw. Beuerlein started to laugh, as did several other players nearby. But Seifert was serious and told the quarterback, "They'll never expect it." Beuerlein looked right in the coach's eyes and said, "I promise I will get you five yards." When Beuerlein announced the plan in the huddle, even his teammates were shocked. They expected the quarterback to change the call to a passing play at the line of scrimmage, but that didn't happen. Beuerlein took the snap and dropped back as if to pass. Then he followed his blockers into the end zone for the win.

X In an era in which most great NFL receivers were well over 6 feet tall, 5-foot-9 Panthers wideout Steve Smith became one of the best of them all with his great speed and compact strength.

playing time as a backup with the New Orleans Saints, but he was certain the young passer was ready for stardom. Fox was particularly impressed with Delhomme's poise and his ability to throw long passes that would open up the offense and keep opposing defenders off balance.

The overall roster changes on both sides of the ball left Carolina fans and players hopeful. "You look around, and you get a very strong feeling that this is the time for us," said defensive end Mike Rucker.

The 2002 season was a breakout year for defensive end Mike Rucker, who tallied double-digit (10) sacks for the first time and scored the first points of his NFL career on a safety. **X**

THE CARDIAC CATS

The Panthers began 2003 with two heart-stopping victories and soon earned the nickname "Cardiac Cats" from local sportswriters. In the season opener, Delhomme came off the bench to spark a 17-point fourth-quarter rally and eke out a 24–23 win over the Jacksonville Jaguars. The winning play was a 12-yard touchdown toss from Delhomme to Proehl with only 16 seconds left in the game. The next week, Panthers defenders blocked a Tampa Bay Buccaneers extra-point attempt with no time remaining to force overtime, then won the game on a 47-yard John Kasay field goal a few minutes later.

The Cardiac Cats kept up the drama, capturing three more exciting contests in a row before suffering their first loss against the Tennessee Titans in Week 6. The rest of the season was just as exciting, as Carolina earned two overtime victories and rallied for last-minute wins in two other games to finish with an 11–5 record and the NFC South Division title. (Carolina had joined the new NFC South when the league was realigned in 2002.)

For only the second time in team history, the Panthers were in the playoffs. Back in 1995, Jerry Richardson had promised Carolina fans that their new team would play in a Super Bowl within 10 years. This was the Panthers' ninth season, and they were determined to keep Richardson's

X With swift rookie halfback DeShaun Foster (pictured) backing up starter Stephen Davis, the Super Bowl-bound Panthers featured the NFL's seventh-ranked rushing attack in 2003.

MEET THE PANTHERS

JAKE DELHOMME

QUARTERBACK
PANTHERS SEASONS: 2003–PRESENT
HEIGHT: 6-FOOT-2
WEIGHT: 215 POUNDS

Jake Delhomme was never the fastest nor the most accurate quarterback in the NFL. Each season, his skill level usually ranked near the middle of all starting quarterbacks in the league. But when it came to engineering a successful fourth-quarter drive to earn a win for the Panthers, Delhomme was truly special. "You have to believe that you have the ability [to perform in the clutch] because, if not, this league will eat you up," Delhomme said. "You have to have confidence to know that you have done this already a few times, and you can do it again." Delhomme showed his confidence in the Panthers' drive to the Super Bowl in 2003: He led the Panthers to victory on the final possession of eight games, including his double-overtime scoring bomb against the St. Louis Rams to clinch the NFC championship. Delhomme gained respect around the league for his performance in 2003 and continued to enhance his reputation in following seasons. Said NFL analyst Merrill Hoge: "He's a big-play quarterback.... He does make plays at critical times in order to help his team win."

promise. It was not going to be an easy task, however.

Carolina had to get past three NFC powerhouses—the Dallas

Cowboys, St. Louis Rams, and Philadelphia Eagles—to earn a

berth in Super Bowl XXXVIII, which was scheduled for February

1, 2004, in Houston, Texas.

The Panthers quickly dispatched the Cowboys 29–10 at

Ericsson Stadium in the opening round, led by John Kasay's

five field goals. Then they battled the Rams in a contest that

went into double-overtime in St. Louis before escaping with a

29–23 win on a long Delhomme-to-Smith touchdown strike.

X The Panthers'
defense overwhelmed
the Cowboys' offense in
their playoff matchup
after the 2003 season,
surrendering only 78
rushing yards.

X Receiver Keary Colbert made the Panthers' passing attack even scarier in 2004, averaging 16 yards per catch and scoring 5 touchdowns as just a rookie.

The following week, the Panthers faced off against the Eagles in Philadelphia for the NFC championship. Giving a pep talk before the title contest, Brentson Buckner exhorted his teammates: "Everyone says we're not supposed to win. But this isn't predetermined. We hit as hard as they do. We practice as hard as they do. I want us to take over Philly. I want us to take the whole city and shut it down!"

The fired-up Panthers did just that. In a defensive struggle, Coach Fox's forces shut down Philadelphia quarterback Donovan McNabb completely, sacking him five times, intercepting three of his passes, and forcing him to

FIGHT FOR LIFE

Carolina players had more than football on their minds during the 2003 season. The same year the club battled all the way to the Super Bowl, two Panthers players were battling for their lives. Their courageous fight inspired the whole team. During preseason training camp, Carolina players learned that starting linebacker Mark Fields and former Panthers star Sam Mills (pictured), now one of the team's assistant coaches, had been diagnosed with cancer. "Everybody was shocked and devastated," said safety Mike Minter. "You hear cancer and you just automatically think, 'that's it.'" But neither Fields nor Mills was giving up, and the team rallied around them. Throughout the season, Panthers players wore a T-shirt under their jerseys that bore the numbers 51 for Mills and 58 for Fields. They played with extra spirit all season, as if to make up for their missing teammates. Fields recovered and played one more year for Carolina in 2004. Sadly, Mills succumbed to the disease and died in April 2005. A bronze statue of Mills today stands in front of Bank of America Stadium, where it continues to inspire the team.

[35]

MUHSIN MUHAMMAD

WIDE RECEIVER
PANTHERS SEASONS: 1996-2004,
2008-PRESENT
HEIGHT: 6-FOOT-2
WEIGHT: 217 POUNDS

When Lansing, Michigan, native Melvin Campbell was only four years old, his father converted to Islam and changed the young boy's name to Muhsin Muhammad. He grew up to be a triple-threat athlete in high school, excelling in football, basketball, and track, and then went on to star on the gridiron for Michigan State University. The Panthers selected Muhammad in the second round of the 1996 NFL Draft and looked to him to open up the club's offensive attack. Muhammad was a big disappointment his first 2 seasons in Carolina, catching just 52 passes. Then, in his third year, he suddenly emerged as one of the league's best receivers. From 1998 to 2004, he averaged more than 1,000 receiving yards per season and caught 43 touchdown passes. Some of the most familiar sounds heard in Ericsson Stadium were shouts of "Moooooose!" when Muhammad made one of his spectacular receptions. Many fans even wore toy moose antlers to games to show their support. Muhammad left Carolina in 2005 to play with the Chicago Bears for three years but was re-signed by the Panthers before the 2008 season.

scramble all afternoon. The end result was a 14–3 Carolina victory and a spot in the Super Bowl two weeks later against the powerful American Football Conference (AFC) champs, the New England Patriots.

That Super Bowl was one of the tightest and most exciting ever. The lead seesawed back and forth, and the two teams were deadlocked at 29–29 after Delhomme hit Proehl with a 12-yard scoring pass with a little more than a minute remaining in regulation. Carolina fans were readying themselves for another overtime thriller when disaster struck. Kasay's kickoff went out of bounds, resulting in a penalty that gave the Patriots excellent field position. New England's star quarterback, Tom Brady, made the most of the break, driving the Pats quickly inside Carolina territory and within range for a winning field goal. Adam Vinatieri's 41-yard kick sealed the win for New England as time ran out.

The Panthers were certain—the way their offense was clicking—that if there had been time for just one more Carolina drive in regulation or overtime, Delhomme would have found a way to lead the team to victory. "We didn't lose," several players remarked sadly after the game. "We just ran out of time."

BATTLING TO STAY ON TOP

Optimism ran high in the Carolinas in the summer of 2004 as the Panthers prepared to defend their NFC crown. Then, in the season opener against the Packers, which was broadcast nationally on Monday Night Football, both Davis and Smith suffered season-ending injuries. With their offense seriously weakened, the Panthers lost that game and six of the next seven. Standing at 1–7, the season seemed to be lost. But Coach Fox used all of his motivational skills to pull the club out of its downward skid. Reserve running back Nick Goings stepped in to carry the rushing load, and Muhsin Muhammad had an All-Pro season with 1,405 receiving yards and 16 touchdowns. The club won six of its last eight games and barely missed the playoffs.

Carolina's comeback in 2004 convinced most football experts that the Panthers would excel in 2005. *Sports Illustrated* even featured the Cats on the cover of its NFL preview issue. That didn't make local fans happy, though, since being on the *Sports Illustrated* cover has often been considered bad luck. As if to prove the point, the Panthers lost two of their first three games. Then the offense began to roar, and the club won its next six contests. Entering the final game of the year, Carolina still needed one more win to reach the playoffs as the NFC Wild Card. Facing the Falcons in Atlanta, the Panthers scored early and kept pouring it on to win 44–11 and qualify for the postseason.

The next week, the Carolina defense completely shut down the favored New York Giants for a 23–0 playoff win. Then the offense—led by Delhomme, Smith, and running back DeShaun Foster—took over the following week in a 29–21 road victory over the Chicago Bears. The Panthers were back in the NFC title game and just one victory away from another Super Bowl appearance. But the team's good fortune came to an abrupt end when the Seattle Seahawks defeated Carolina handily, 34–14. "I don't know if we ran out of gas," said Coach Fox. "I'm not sure what the problem was. Their defense played tremendous. They stopped us cold."

The letdown from the loss to Seattle seemed to carry over to the 2006 season. The Panthers played inconsistently all year, baffling fans as they followed impressive wins with disappointing losses. They finished the year 8–8, one victory shy of a berth in the playoffs.

TWICE IN A LIFETIME

When Panthers wide receiver Ricky Proehl caught a 12-yard touchdown pass from Jake Delhomme with just over a minute to go in Super Bowl XXXVIII to forge a tie with the New England Patriots, most Carolina fans were ecstatic. But Proehl was a little worried. Two years earlier as a member of the St. Louis Rams, Proehl had caught a game-tying pass against New England with 1:37 to go in Super Bowl XXXVI. In the time remaining, Pats quarterback Tom Brady drove his team directly down the field, and placekicker Adam Vinatieri won the game for New England with a long field goal. This time, Proehl watched fearfully as the same events seemed to be recurring. "It must be a nightmare," he told himself. "Déjà vu was happening all over again." After John Kasay's misdirected kickoff, Brady took charge, setting up another last-second, game-winning field goal by Vinatieri. Following the game, Proehl lamented, "You make a couple of big plays at the end, like I did [this time and] two years ago, and you're high as a kite. Then, a minute later, it doesn't mean anything."

TEN-YEAR ANNIVERSARY

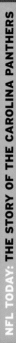

The Carolina Panthers haven't had a long history, but it has been eventful. To celebrate the club's 10th anniversary in 2005, the team set up a special multimedia section on its Web site at www.panthers.com. Those accessing the Web site could watch video interviews with key figures in the team's history; relive exciting and memorable moments; and compare their own lists of the top players, games, and plays in team history with those selected by the club's media relations staff. The top-ranking game and play both occurred on January 10, 2004, when the Panthers took on the St. Louis Rams for the NFC championship. That game was tied 23–23 at the end of the first overtime period. Then, on the first play of double-overtime, quarterback Jake Delhomme connected with receiver Steve Smith (pictured) for a 69-yard touchdown score. Other top plays included receiver Muhsin Muhammad's 85-yard reception in Super Bowl XXXVIII (the longest offensive play in Super Bowl history) and linebacker Sam Mills's interception and touchdown run against the New York Jets that ensured the team's first-ever win in 1995.

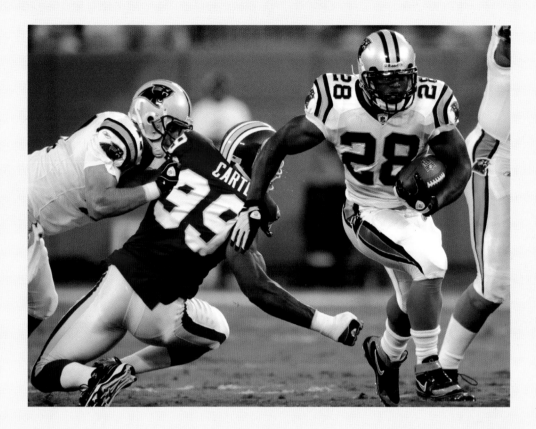

Then the team's offense suffered a big blow when
Delhomme and Goings went down with season-ending injuries
early in 2007. Despite strong efforts by Julius Peppers and
young linebackers Thomas Davis and Jon Beason on defense,
the Panthers couldn't put enough points on the board to
win consistently, finishing the season 7–9. In 2008, though,
the Cats were back. Behind a healthy Delhomme and running
backs Jonathan Stewart and DeAngelo Williams—a dynamic
one-two rushing punch nicknamed "Smash and Dash"—the
Panthers streaked to a 12–4 record and earned a first-round

X Carolina looked
to continue its great
rushing tradition by
selecting bruising
halfback Jonathan
Stewart with the 13th
overall pick of the 2008
NFL Draft.

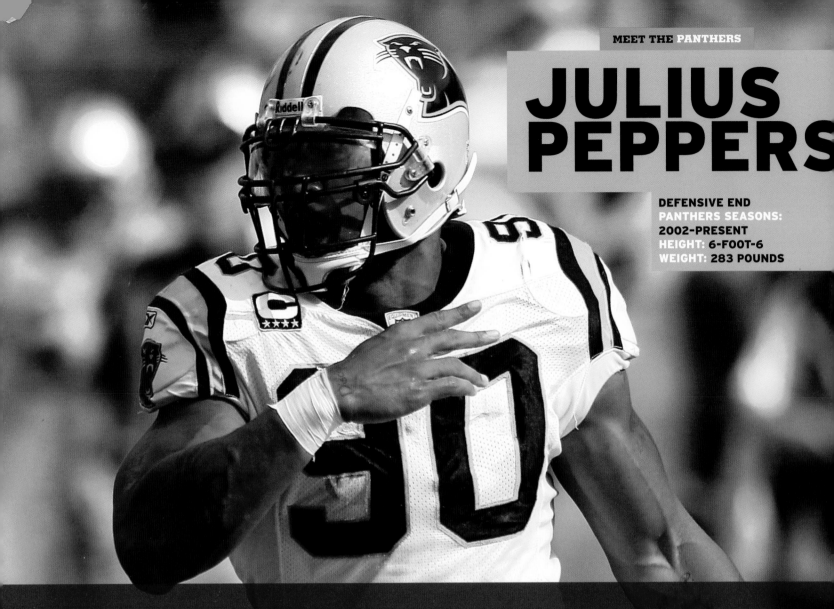

JULIUS PEPPERS

**DEFENSIVE END
PANTHERS SEASONS:
2002-PRESENT
HEIGHT: 6-FOOT-6
WEIGHT: 283 POUNDS**

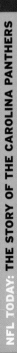

When Julius Peppers arrived at his first Panthers training camp, veteran offensive lineman Chris Terry decided to test out the cocky rookie during a pass rushing and blocking drill. Terry moved forward to pound Peppers with a powerful block, but the two men never made contact. Instead, Peppers stood up, shifted his body quickly, and slipped right past his blocker. If there had been a quarterback in the drill, Peppers would have sacked him easily. Panthers assistant coach Paul Boudreau commented, "Carolina has never had anyone in franchise history like this guy." Peppers's unusual combination of speed, mobility, and size helped him become the NFL's Defensive Rookie of the Year in 2002. He followed that up with three consecutive Pro Bowl appearances from 2004 through 2006. Shy and quiet off the field, Peppers seldom said anything during a game either. Instead, he put his full concentration into rushing the quarterback and making devastating tackles. Explaining his style, Peppers said, "You've got to be disciplined. You have to be under control going in there but be aggressive at the same time."

bye in the playoffs. But then, inexplicably, Carolina came out flat in its second-round game against the Arizona Cardinals, losing at home, 33–13, in a stunning upset.

Some 20 years after Jerry Richardson first began dreaming about establishing a professional football team in the Carolinas, the Panthers have proven to be one of the most successful clubs in the NFL. The team that set league records as an expansion franchise not so long ago is today hoping to find a permanent place among the NFL's elite. As the Panthers continue their hunt for an NFL crown, fans in both North and South Carolina should have plenty to roar about.

With their defense returning to form as one of the toughest in football, the 2008 Panthers rose up again as a force in the NFC South. **X**

INDEX